The Macmillan Company
866 Third Avenue, New York, New York 10022
Collier-Macmillan Canada Ltd., Toronto, Ontario
Library of Congress Catalog Card Number: 79–117960
First Printing
PRINTED IN GREAT BRITAIN

Greetings FROM DOWN UNDER : M. Sasek

KANGAROO PAWS

THIS IS AUSTRALIA

The Macmillan Company

© M. SASEK, 1970

The man responsible

Captain James Cook is sometimes said to be the discoverer of Australia, although it was probably the Dutch who actually discovered it, early in the 17th century. Cook landed there in 1770 and promptly declared the present State of New South Wales a British colony. His ship, the *Endeavour*, was on a scientific mission. The first British settlers came to Australia 18 years later. Most of them were in chains—they were convicts.

Australia is:
the biggest island or the smallest continent; the first continent to be formed —and the last to be discovered; a land as large as the U.S. without Alaska (almost 3 million square miles), with a population not much larger than Tokyo's (12 million); and where Christmas is a summer holiday.

An Australian Qantas bird after a round-the-world flight is homing in on Sydney's International Airport near Botany Bay where Cook landed on his

botanical expedition. Sydney, Australia's biggest, oldest, and most colourful city, is the capital of the State of New South Wales. New South Wales is as large as the American states of Texas and Virginia put together. Half of its population, or about 2,700,000 people, live in Sydney.

This was how Sydney looked 70 years after Cook landed.

And this is Sydney today.

Bent Street

Australia Square Tower
is a round tower in
Australia Square.

chool uniforms

Harbour Bridge (440 ft. high)

More than 100,000 vehicles cross the eight-lane bridge every day. In the morning rush hour, six lanes accommodate the city-bound traffic. In the evening, when the tide of traffic reverses, so do the lanes, and six lanes now serve the outbound vehicles.

The sail-shaped Opera House in the harbour, designed by the Danish architect, Joern Utzon, is still under construction. When finished, it will have six performance areas and will seat 5,440 people.

"Sydney lace" is the
name of the cast-iron railings of
balconies you can see in the terraced
streets in the Paddington area. The wrought iron
originally served as ship's ballast. Some of today's "lace" saw
service on a ship, but much of it is imitation.

Kings Cross

You see the part of Sydney
—most colourful

—most cosmopolitan and flowerful

—most painlessly artistic

—most humorous

when you cross Kings Cross.

One meets one's first Australian animals in the city's Taronga Zoo. And they are the strangest lot you'll ever see! Birds that don't fly or sing, quadrupeds who use their tails as a fifth leg. Some of the world's most primitive species survive in Australia.

Australia's goodwill ambassador.
The whole world loves him.

The kangaroo is born only one inch long, naked and blind, and he climbs through his mother's fur into her pouch, where he stays for about four months. The young one is called "Joey", while the leader of a kangaroo herd is called "The old man". And a very strict old man he is: any younger kangaroo who challenges his authority has a fight on his paws.

Kangaroo family

The tree kangaroo uses his tail only for balance

The wallaby

The rat kangaroo

he emu is Australia's biggest
rd (not counting Qantas jets).
ut unlike Australia's inter-
ational airline, the emu does not
y. A marathon runner, however,
ould have a hard time keeping
p with him on the ground: he
ns at 30 miles per hour.

Another non-flyer is the
Australian penguin,
who can be all of ten
inches small.

The white stilt boasts his long
legs.

The black swans boast
their long necks.

The little white
ones are called
cygnets.

Mr. Kookaburra is happy all day long: he spends his life laughing, but cannot sing a song.

That's what Australian children say of him, but why shouldn't he be happy? He is known as the world's biggest kingfisher, and he is also a formidable snake killer. His nickname is "the laughing jackass".

The wombat is as big as a pig. And as lazy. He spends his days sleeping in his burrow and his nights eating roots and grass.

The echidna is a spiny ant-eater. He is hatched out of an egg like a chick, then suckles his mother's milk like a kitten.

The lyrebird is as artistic as his name. He is a mimic and a dancer. He can imitate not only the calls of other birds, but also the sound of woodchopping.

Platypus looks as if he were forever unable to decide what he wants to be: he has a beak like a bird, he swims under water like a fish, he has fur like a kangaroo, lays eggs, but suckles his young.

The gentle koala is one of the most charming Australians. But he is also a determined individualist and a non-drinker. His name in the language of the aborigines means "not drinking water". He is a gourmet; he feeds on the leaves of only seven out of 500 different kinds of gum trees. And if he looks sleepy, that's because he is, in day-time: he is mainly nocturnal. Born less than an inch long, he lives at first in his mother's pouch, which opens back-wards, and later spends the rest of his childhood hanging around her neck.

Canberra (population 119,000) is the capital of all Australia. After a Federation of Australian States was achieved in 1901, an independent district called The Australian Capital Territory (A.C.T.) was carved out of the State of New South Wales for its site. It is an artificially created city. Even its lake is man-made. It is named Burley Griffin Lake after the American architect whose master plan for Canberra was selected out of many.

Extraordinary attention is paid in Canberra to public parks and private gardens. Anyone who buys a house in the city gets trees for his garden free from the government.

Canberra skyline

Civic Square and Theatre Centre with a statue of Ethos, representing the spirit of the community.

The National Library on the bank of Burley Griffin Lake has been finished only since 1968, and is remarkable for its beautiful exterior and interior design.

The Law Courts

The Australian political system resembles that of Great Britain: there is a Parliament, and the government is headed by a Prime Minister. Since Australia is a member of the British Commonwealth of Nations, its sovereign is the British monarch.
The Commonwealth of Australia comprises six States and eight Territories. The States are: New South Wales, Victoria, Queensland, South Australia, Western Australia, and Tasmania. The Territories are: The Australian Capital Territory, The Northern Territory, Papua-New Guinea, Norfolk Island, Cocos Island, Christmas Island, Heard and MacDonald Islands, and Australian Antarctic Territory.

Australian coat of arms

Every scenic place in the vicinity of Canberra has a picnic area with gas barbecue pits for weekenders.

This is the house of the first governor of the State of Victoria. Built in 1939, it was a much more modest residence than governors' mansions are today. Unlike state governors in the U.S., Australian governors are not elected officials and in no way enter local politics, their functions being mainly ceremonial as representatives of the Queen.

Victoria is the smallest mainland state, but a very densely populated one, where more than one quarter of the entire population lives. The capital of Victoria is Melbourne. It lies on the Yarra River whose name in the aboriginals' tongue means "everflowing". This is the heliport.

Melbourne is the centre of finance, commerce and mining. But not all money goes into business. Horse races are very popular, as in all of Australia, the main event being the Melbourne Cup.

St. Peter's Cathedral

The population of Melbourne is just over two million, which makes it the second largest city of Australia. It also has a reputation as Australia's most "British" city.

Burke Street

Don't worry, he's no longer at large. Ned Kelly, the famed outlaw, or bushranger as they called him, was hanged in Melbourne in 1880.

Shopping arcades are numerous in all Australian cities. The best known in Melbourne is the Royal Arcade. (The statues are Gog and Magog.)

Modern Australian architecture is boldly experimental.

Myer Music Bowl, an open-air auditorium, can seat 200,000 music-lovers (but that's counting those on the lawn outside as well).

The Royal Botanical Garden in Melbourne is one of the most beautiful in the world, as well as one of the largest.

Hobart, the capital of Tasmania, at the foot of Mount Wellington, is Australia's southernmost city. It is also its second oldest colony. Tasmania is an island, separated from the mainland by Bass Strait. It has higher rainfall than any other Australian state. It is mountainous, lush, and green, covered by impenetrable forests fascinating to the naturalist. It is mild in summer and cool in winter. It is a paradise island and, as a paradise should, it grows beautiful apples.

But here comes the Tasmanian devil. He is a meat-eating marsupial, a distant relative of the kangaroo, and he is not exactly a handsome devil.

31

Lenah Valley
Every house in Hobart's suburbs features its own little botanical garden.

Mount Wellington is 4,165 ft. high and is snow-capped in winter. In the foreground is the Cascade Brewery, the only establishment in Hobart permitted to draw the limpid mountain water, which it transforms into cascades of beer. The Great Australian Thirst is assuaged with beer.

But here comes the Tasmanian devil. He is a meat-eating marsupial, a distant relative of the kangaroo, and he is not exactly a handsome devil.

Hobart has one of the deepest harbours anywhere. It is in Hobart's harbour that the tough annual 740-mile yacht race from Sydney ends.

Liverpool Street. Welcome to "Westend Shopping Spree!" The swap shop is just what it says it is: it lets you swap the things you don't need for the ones you do need.

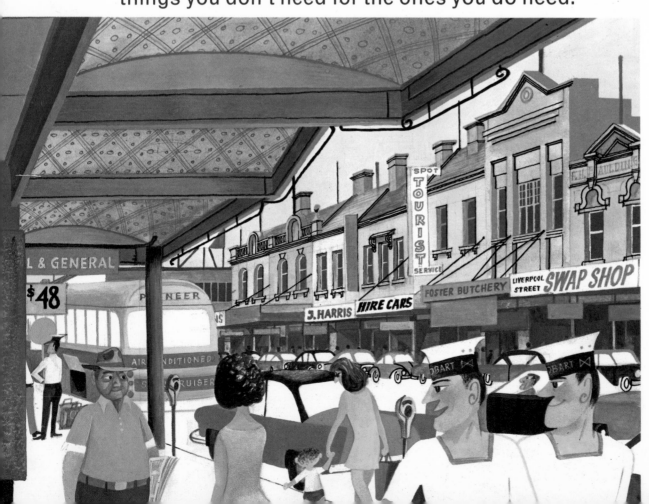

CAT AND FIDDLE SQUARE

CHARLES

Cat and Fiddle Square is where Hobart
children love to go shopping with mother
to see the cat fiddle, which it does every
hour.

One-man protest march

Lenah Valley
Every house in Hobart's suburbs features its own little botanical garden.

Mount Wellington is 4,165 ft. high and is snow-capped in winter. In the foreground is the Cascade Brewery, the only establishment in Hobart permitted to draw the limpid mountain water, which it transforms into cascades of beer. The Great Australian Thirst is assuaged with beer.

Port Arthur, 62 miles from Hobart, now stands in ruins. But in the last century it provided accommodation for some 30,000 new arrivals to Australia. Founded in 1830, and named after British Governor Arthur, it was considered the latest in contemporary design. No, it was not a hotel. It was a penitentiary.

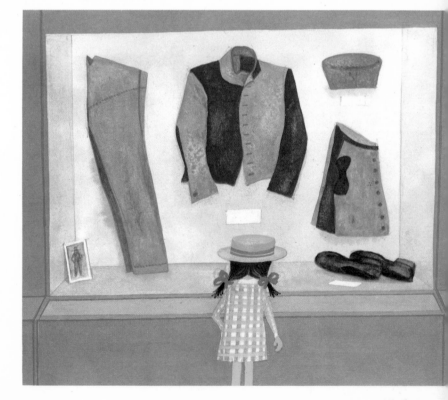

Much attention was evidently also paid to fashion design at Port Arthur. This was a lifer's uniform.

But Port Arthur's design for living was something else again.

Offences	Number of Lashes in each Year							
	1830	1831	1832	1833	1834	1835	1836	1837
...conding	37763	51218	49503	53038	47111	50737	42441	31735
...enting	13295	15801	13552	26552	34833	39872	38536	3644
...obedience of orders	13158	2463	18395	30731	30757	35848	35909	27601
...nkedness	7233	993	7279	14256	15738	26809	35612	42643
...tious or Insubordinate			...792	908				

Today, a ball is no longer dragged on a chain: it is rolled along a bowling green . . .

. . . or a green billiard table.

In the world of sports, life-savers hold a special place of honour. Many a swimmer Down Under would have stayed down under without their prompt intervention. About 25,000 of them man Australian beaches, volunteers and crack swimmers all.

Australia has thousands of miles of beaches, and the most famous of them are in Queensland.

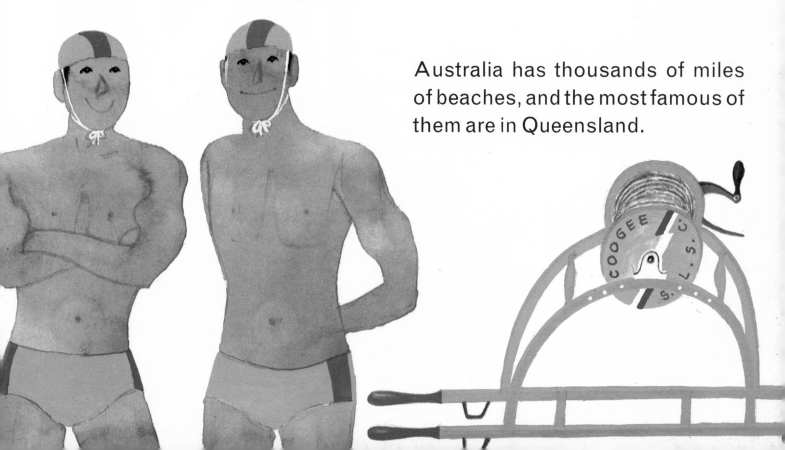

Queensland has coral reefs, tropical rain forests, mountains—more varied scenery than any other state. It also has many other things: coal, copper, wool, oil, silver, bauxite, timber . . . you name it.

Brisbane, the capital of Queensland, started out as a very exclusive settlement. For many years no one was allowed to live closer to it than 50 miles. It was a penal colony.

Although today's Brisbane has only just over 750,000 inhabitants, it is the fifth largest metropolitan area in the world. This is due to the fact that most of it consists of individual family houses with gardens.

View from the Storey Bridge
Brisbane's harbour is 12 miles away, but ships can come right up into the middle of the city on Brisbane River, which snakes through it.

Situated at the edge of the tropics, Brisbane does not grow tropical trees only in botanical gardens. These, in front of the ANZAC Memorial, are called baobabs or boabs or just what they look like: bottle trees. (ANZAC means Australian and New Zealand Army Corps.)

Poinciana trees in Kemp Place

Two sanctuaries in the vicinity of Brisbane are a must for tourists:

the Currumbin Bird Sanctuary where they can feed bread and honey to rainbow lorikeet—

and the Lone Pine Koala Sanctuary where they can see a koala dog-ride or have their picture taken with a sweet little Australian named Susie.

Darwin, the capital of Northern Territory, is in the northernmost part of Australia. The Northern Territory is as large as six Great Britains but has a population of only about 69,000, including both white Australians and aborigines, half of whom live in Darwin. A large part of the Northern Territory is in the torrid zone, an area of broken, eroded mountain ranges and wide plains, sparsely overgrown with low eucalyptus trees and semi-desert grasses. Its principal industries are cattle raising and mining.

Darwin is so near the Top End, the most tropical coastal strip of Australia, that one has to watch for falling coconuts on one's way to the mailbox.

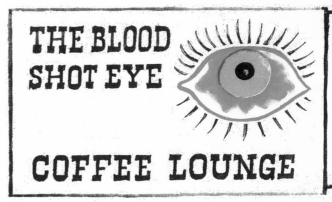

THE BLOOD SHOT EYE

COFFEE LOUNGE

PLEASE NOTE

GUN SHOP IS NOW IN THE SALVATION ARMY BUILDING MITCHELL ST.

Darwin is a frontier town.
On a Sunday morning Smith Street, the main shopping
artery, resembles a setting for a western.

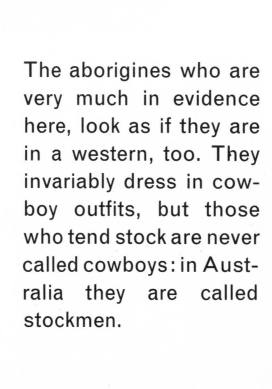

The aborigines who are
very much in evidence
here, look as if they are
in a western, too. They
invariably dress in cow-
boy outfits, but those
who tend stock are never
called cowboys: in Aust-
ralia they are called
stockmen.

Although some aborigines have exchanged the spear for the cattle prod, in more remote areas others still live as they may have done in the Stone Age, with their legends, their dances, their wood carvings and their bark paintings.

Botanical garden in Darwin.

Alice Springs, the Red Heart of Australia

1,000 miles south of Darwin, the town called Alice Springs or The Alice (sometimes known as the Centre for short) is in the middle of the Great Australian Outback—the merciless, arid, hot, reddish bush and desert.

This is the view of The Alice from the ANZAC Memorial.

Parsons Street

The eucalyptus, called the gum tree, grows everywhere in Australia: here one grows right in the middle of the street—

—while others grow right in the middle of the Todd River, or what is Todd River in the rainy season. But even if there is no water in the Todd River, Alice Springers hold a regatta anyway: it is more fun without water.

In Alice Springs, most days are trainless as well as rainless. A train comes in from, and leaves for, Adelaide only twice a week, and only then the railway station comes to life. But this engine never goes anywhere. It stands in front of the station and keeps the station-master company on trainless days.

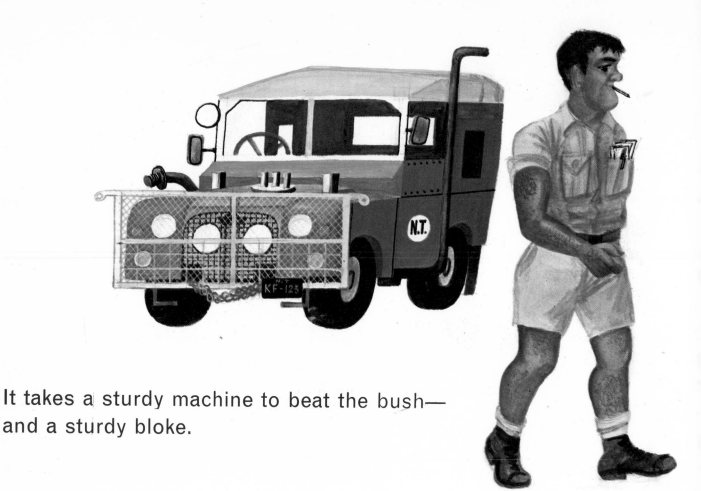

It takes a sturdy machine to beat the bush— and a sturdy bloke.

Forty years ago, only 27 people lived here. But since a railway was built to The Alice, the town's population has grown to 6,000, including 800 aborigines.

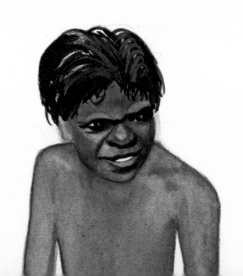

Ayer's Rock

This gigantic sandstone monolith, rising to a height of 1,143 ft. from the plain 300 miles southwest of Alice Springs, is over five miles in circumference. The aborigines have left rock paintings in the caves at its base.

This is The Climb, the only way to get to the top.

The coloration of the cliff face changes suddenly, several times a day, according to light conditions and reflection from the surface, depending on the amount of moisture in the air.

It seems from the plane that there is nothing in this never-never land except gum trees and snakes. But there's a lot hidden underground.

This is the cast of the "Welcome Stranger" gold nugget. Its weight is 2,280 ounces and it was found near the surface on February 5, 1860, in Victoria. Besides gold, Australia has silver, copper, nickel, uranium and other ores; it has coal fields and diamond fields. As for opals, they are almost as plentiful as mushrooms. They are the national gemstones.

As good as gold: a Merino ram can fetch 15,000 dollars—nothing to be sheepish about—if his jealous owner will sell him.

There is not even a second-hand Merino in this shop.

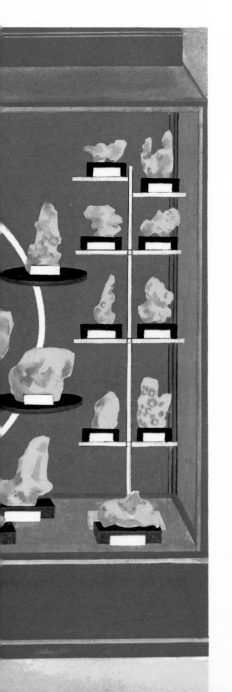

Adelaide is the capital of South Australia.
This is the view from Light's Vision, named after Colonel William Light, Adelaide's founding father. The city is surrounded with parks. Although two-thirds of the state is desert, it is an important agricultural area. South Australia also has large vineyards, and most of the country's wine comes from there—and, incidentally, most of its salt.

This park on the Torrens River, which flows through Adelaide, is also a bird sanctuary. Folk are welcome, as long as they don't disturb the fowl.

St. Peter's Cathedral

Adelaide is a modern city with a colonial charm. In colonial times, it scored many an Australian first. It was Australia's first municipality and its first capital to have a telegraph cable link with London.

Perth, the capital of Western Australia.

This is the view of the city from King's Park, a thousand-acre area atop Mt. Eliza, overlooking the Swan River.

Western Australia — not surprisingly the state farthest west—is also the largest state, comprising almost a third of the country.

The growth of Perth was slow, until gold was discovered in Western Australia at the end of last century. Since then, the mining industry in Western Australia kept growing, and so did Perth. From a settlement of 300 in 1829, it grew to a city of 500,000.

The Karri tree grows taller than any Australian—also taller than any other member of the eucalyptus family. This karri log in King's Park is 106 ft. long, 363 years old, and its bottom girth is 24 ft.

St. Andrew's Presbyterian Church and the Superannuation Building.

London Court looks like a tiny piece of 16th-century England transplanted Down Under. But it is not as old as it looks. It dates back only to 1937—fairly old for Australia, anyway.

Barracks Arch, left standing for memory's sake, is the result of a compromise between tradition and progress: it is a segment of an old Tudor-style barracks.

Old Mill was built in 1835 and has been restored to its original appearance. It is one of the few remains in Perth of pioneer days. But those days are not far behind, and they have left their imprint on the Australian's character: independent, self-reliant, easygoing and hospitable, he has a sense of Australia as a unique place in which a man has a better chance to work out his destiny than anywhere else.